Welcome to your new How To Draw book!

This book is full of lots of fun pictures and amazing animals for you to draw!

Some of the pages will show you the picture and how to draw it step-by-step. Just copy each step and watch the animal or picture come to life as you draw it !

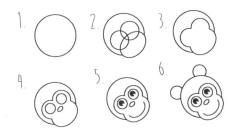

Other pages will show you how to copy the picture using a grid, just copy the lines in each box, one by one, to complete the picture. Once you have tried it using the grid, you can try to draw it without the lines !

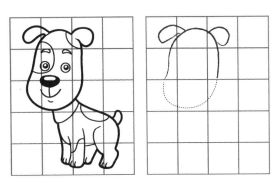

Have Fun!

COPY THE HAMSTER

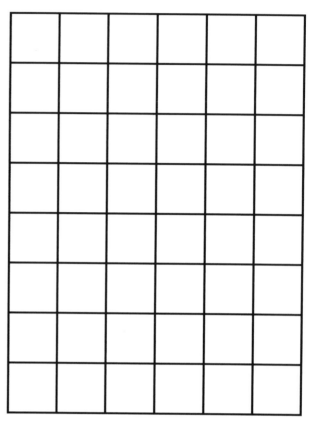

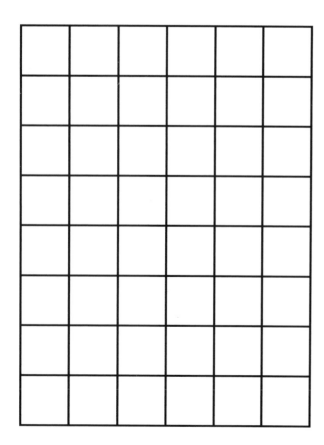

THE GORGEOUS
How To
Draw
Book
FOR GIRLS

A Fun and Easy Step by Step
Drawing Book!

Elizabeth James

First published in 2016 by Kyle Craig Publishing

Copyright © 2016 Kyle Craig Publishing

Editor: Alison McNicol

Design: Elizabeth James, Julie Anson, Alison McNicol, Shutterstock, Inc.

ISBN: 978-1-78595-247-0

A CIP record for this book is available from the British Library.

A Kyle Craig Publication

www.kyle-craig.com

BIRD

YOUR TURN TO DRAW

1.

2.

3.

4.

5.

6.

7.

8.

9.

10.

11.

COPY THE LADYBUG

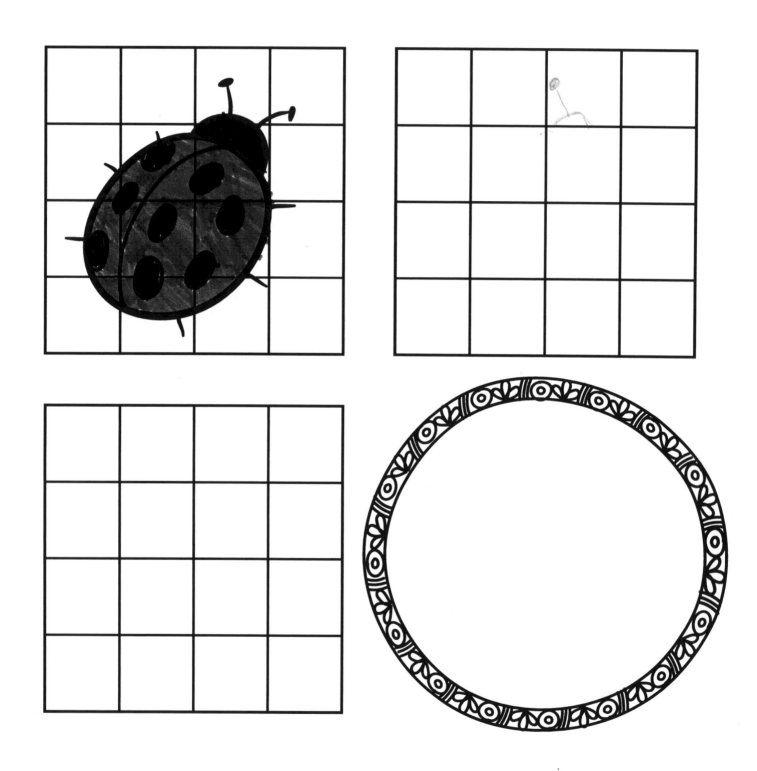

BOW

1. 2. 3.
4. 5. 6.
7. 8. 9.

YOUR TURN TO DRAW

BUTTERFLY

YOUR TURN TO DRAW

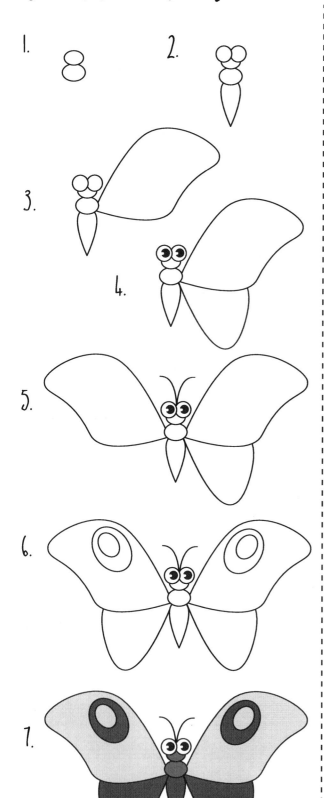

1.

2.

3.

4.

5.

6.

7.

COPY THE OWL

COPY THE BUTTERFLY

DRAGONFLY

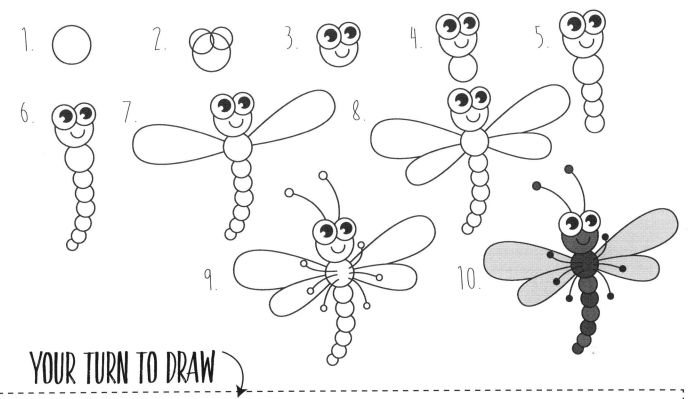

1. 2. 3. 4. 5.
6. 7. 8. 9. 10.

YOUR TURN TO DRAW

EASTER BASKET

1. 2. 3. 4.
5. 6. 7. 8.
9. 10. 11. 12.

YOUR TURN TO DRAW

COPY THE PANDA

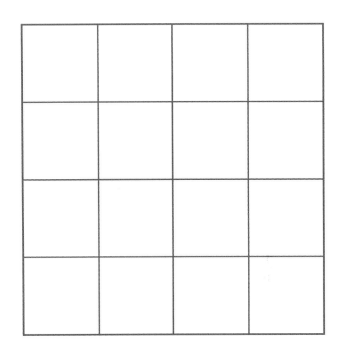

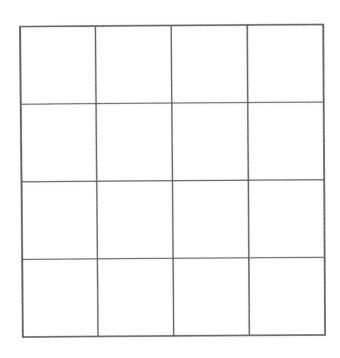

COPY THE DOG

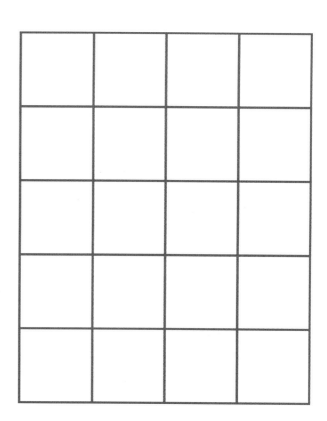

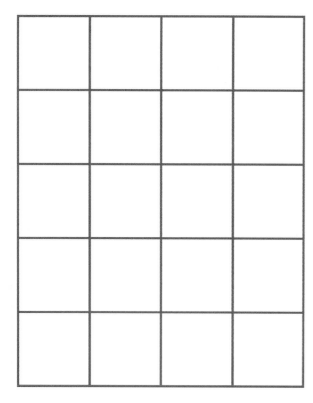

DOG

1. DRAW EARS, ...

2. THE HEAD, ...

3. THE NOSE, ...

4. THE BACK ...

5. ...AND ADD THE TAIL!

6. DRAW SOME FEET, ...

7. NEXT EYES...

8. AND THE MOUTH!

9. NOW, ADD SOME DETAILS AND ...

10.

COPY THE WOLF

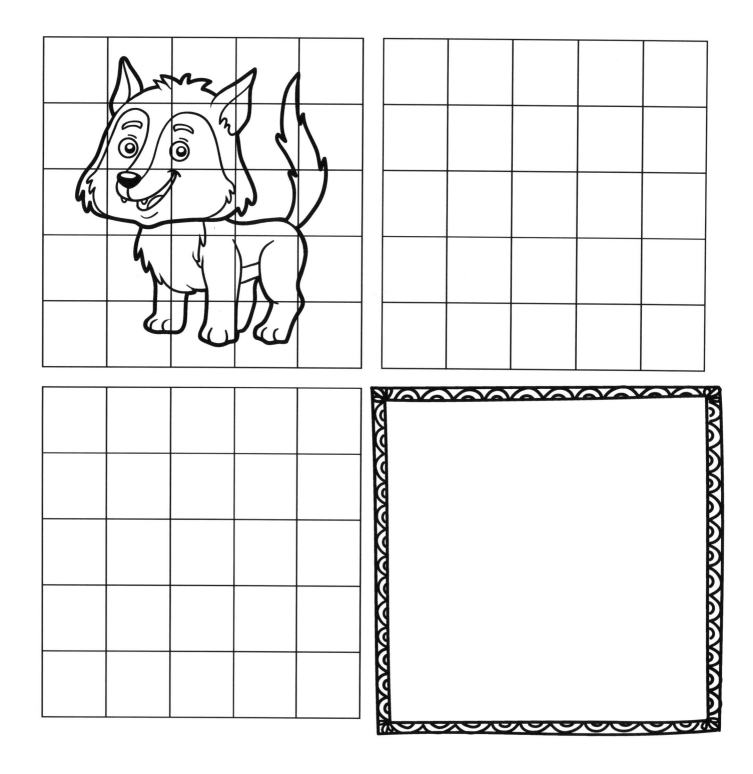

RABBIT

YOUR TURN TO DRAW ↘

1. DRAW EARS, ...

2. THE HEAD, ...

3. THE NOSE, ...

4. THE BACK ...

...AND ADD THE TAIL!

5.

6. DRAW SOME FEET, ...

7. NEXT EYES...
AND THE MOUTH!

8. NOW, ADD SOME DETAILS
AND ...

9.

DEER

YOUR TURN TO DRAW

1. DRAW HORNS, ...

2. EARS, ...

3. THE HEAD, ...

4. THE BACK ...

5. ...AND ADD THE TAIL!

6. DRAW SOME LEGS!

7. NEXT EYES...
AND THE MOUTH!

8. NOW, ADD SOME DETAILS
AND ...

9.

COPY THE TURTLE

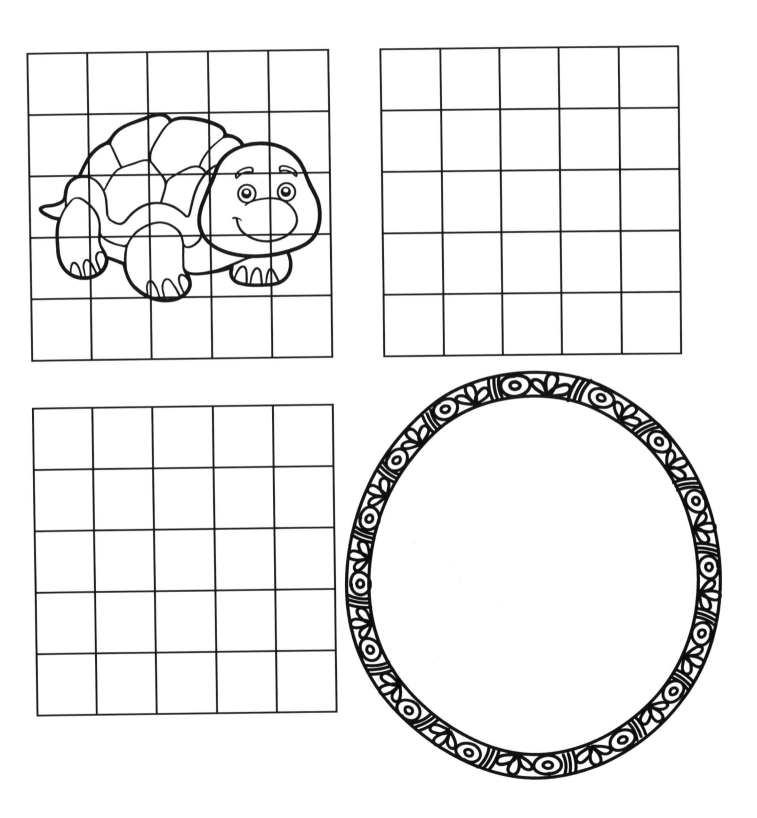

FLOWER

1.

2.

3.

4.

5.

6.

7.

8.

9.

YOUR TURN TO DRAW

COPY THE LAMB

FOX

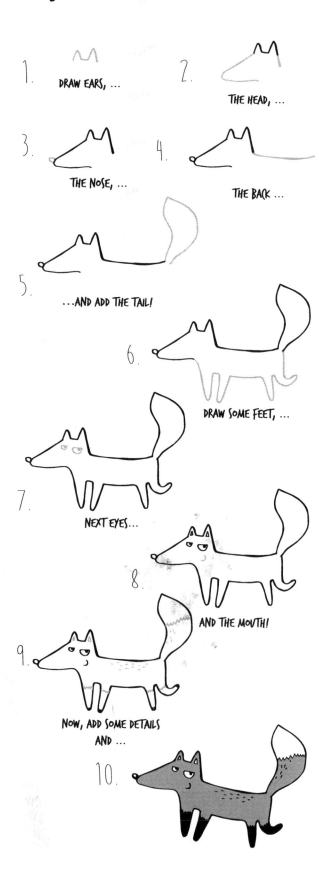

1. DRAW EARS, ...

2. THE HEAD, ...

3. THE NOSE, ...

4. THE BACK ...

5. ...AND ADD THE TAIL!

6. DRAW SOME FEET, ...

7. NEXT EYES...

8. AND THE MOUTH!

9. NOW, ADD SOME DETAILS AND ...

10.

COPY THE HEDGEHOG

COPY THE PENGUIN

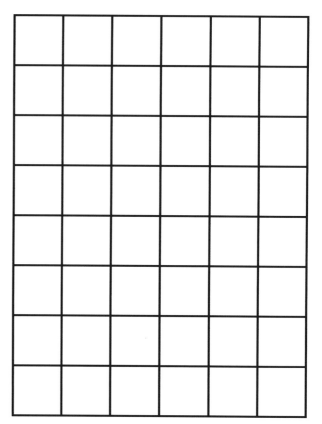

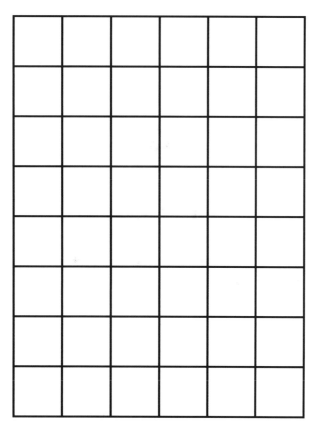

HAT

CAT

YOUR TURN TO DRAW ⤵

1. DRAW EARS, ...

2. THE HEAD, ...

3. THE BACK ...

4. ...AND ADD THE TAIL!

5. DRAW SOME FEET, ...

6. NEXT EYES...

7. AND THE MOUTH!

8. NOW, ADD SOME DETAILS AND ...

Meow Meow

9.

COPY THE CHICK

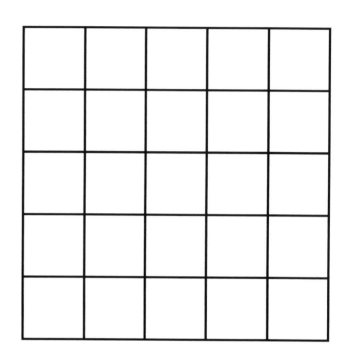

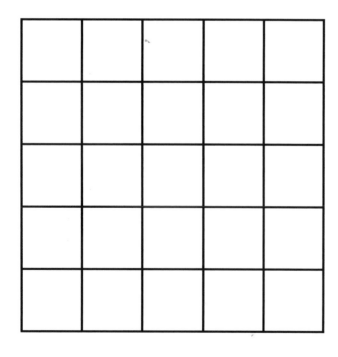

HOUSE

YOUR TURN TO DRAW

1.

2.

3.

4.

5.

6.

7.

8.

9.

10.

11.

12.

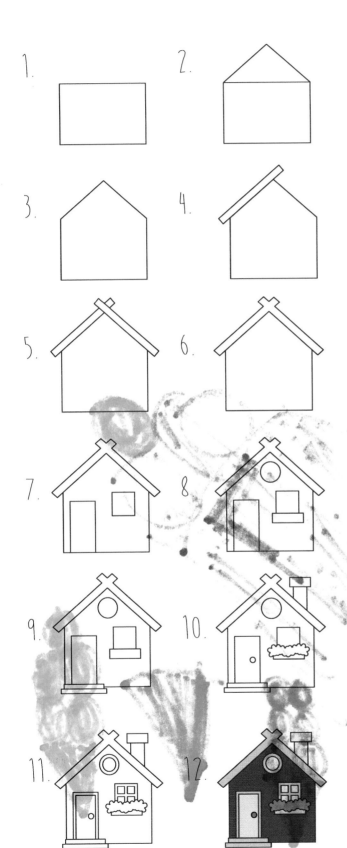

ICE CREAM

YOUR TURN TO DRAW

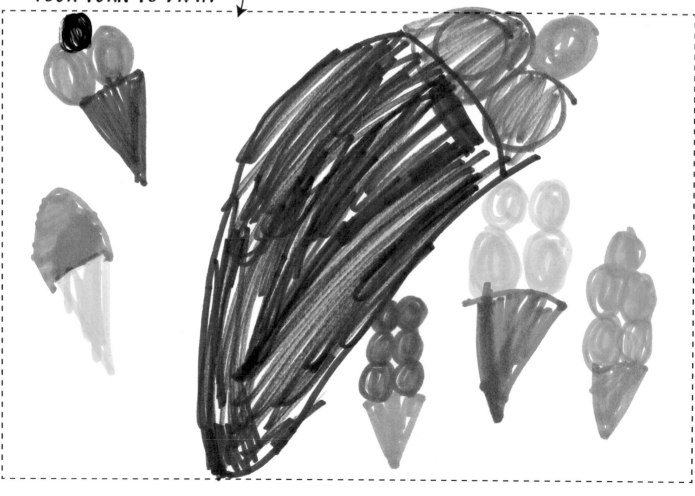

KOALA

YOUR TURN TO DRAW

1.

2.

3.

4.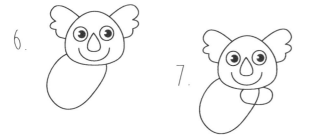

5.

6.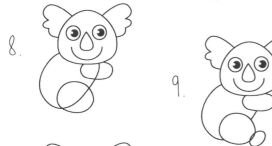

7.

8.

9.

10.

11.

12.

13.

BEAR

YOUR TURN TO DRAW

1. DRAW EARS, ...

2. THE HEAD, ...

3. THE BACK ...

4. ...AND ADD THE TAIL!

5. DRAW SOME FEET, ...

6. NEXT EYES...

7. AND THE MOUTH!

8. NOW, ADD SOME DETAILS AND ...

9.

COPY THE MONKEY

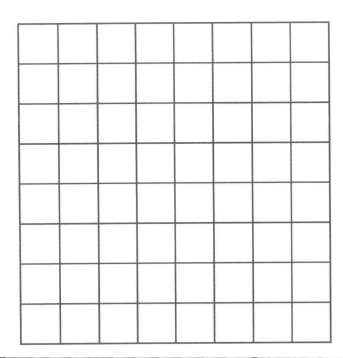
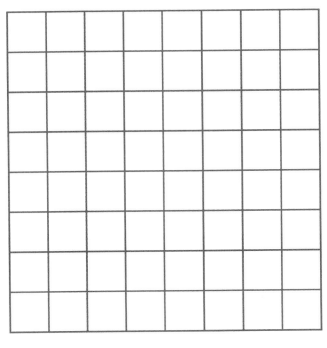

LOVE HEART

1. 2. 3.

4. 5. 6.

7. 8. 9.

YOUR TURN TO DRAW

COPY THE PARROT

MONKEY

YOUR TURN TO DRAW ⟶

1.
2.
3.
4.
5.
6.
7.
8.
9.
10.
11.
12.

COPY THE LION

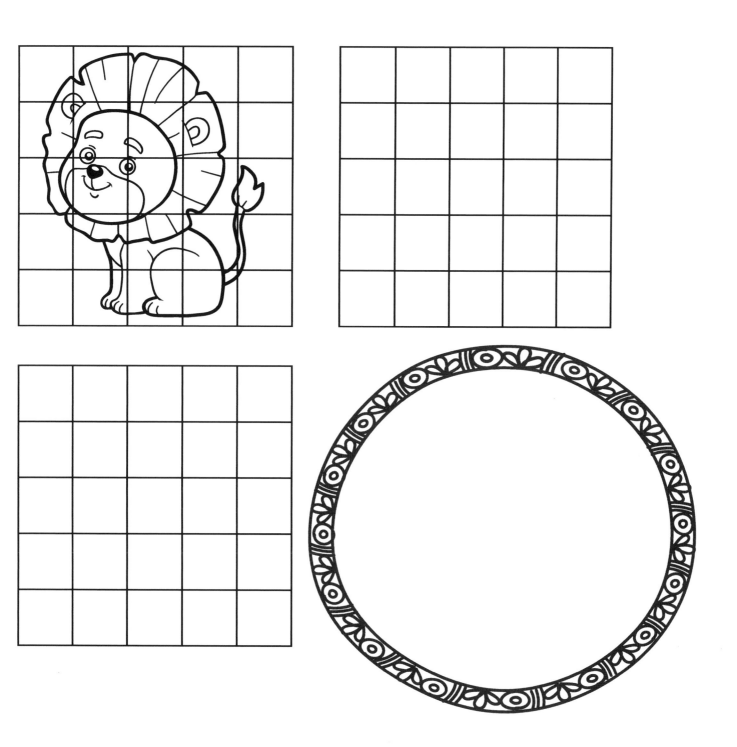

MOUSE

1.
2.
3.
4.
5.
6.
7.
8.
9.

YOUR TURN TO DRAW

COPY THE SHEEP

OWL

1.
2.
3.
4.
5.
6.
7.
8.
9.

YOUR TURN TO DRAW

COPY THE STRAWBERRY

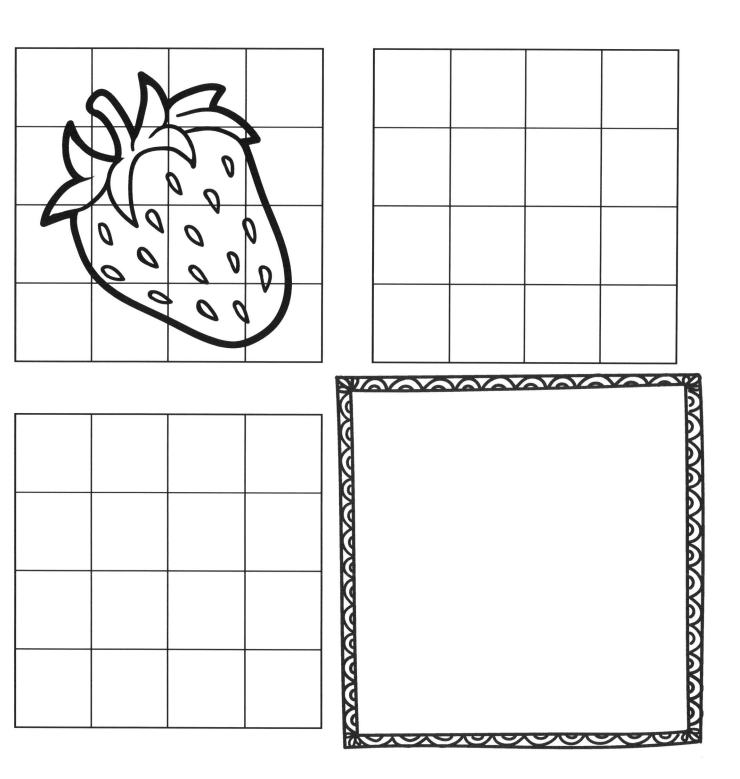

PENGUIN

1. 2. 3. 4.

5. 6. 7.

YOUR TURN TO DRAW

COPY THE COW

COPY SANTA CLAUS

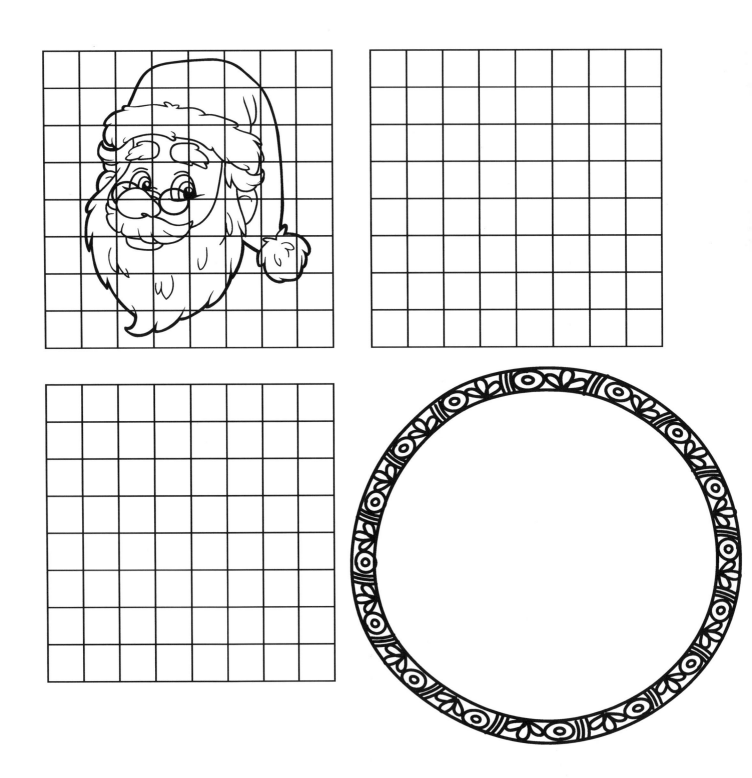

PuPPY

YOUR TURN TO DRAW

1.
2.
3.
4.
5.
6.
7.

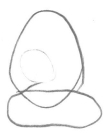

ROSE

 1.

2.

3.

4.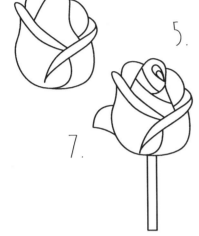

5.

6.

7.

8.

9.

YOUR TURN TO DRAW

COPY THE BUNNY

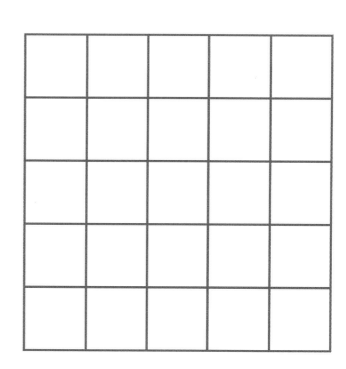

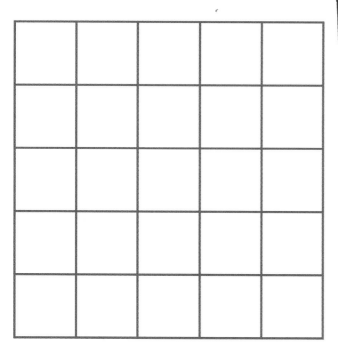

SNAIL

1.　2.　3.　4.

5.　6.

7.　8.

YOUR TURN TO DRAW

COPY THE KITTEN

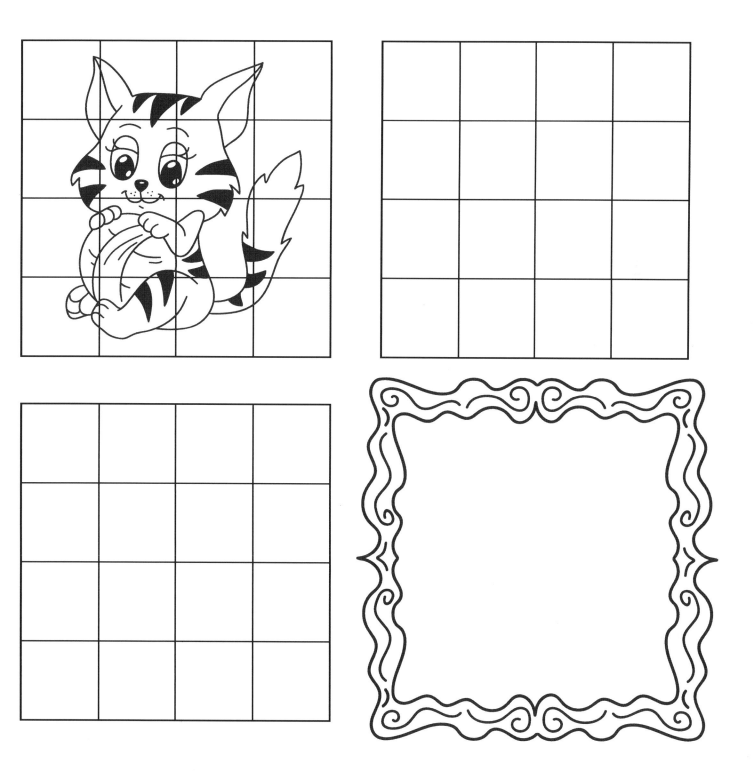

SUN

1. 2. 3.
4. 5. 6.

YOUR TURN TO DRAW

COPY THE CHRISTMAS TREE

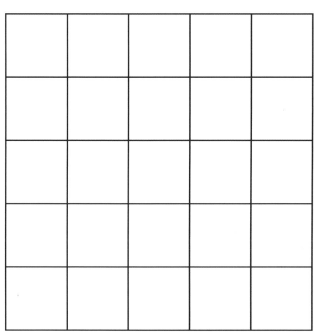

COPY THE MOUSE

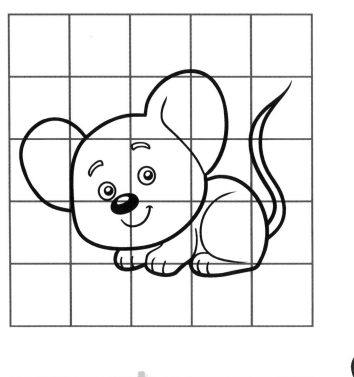

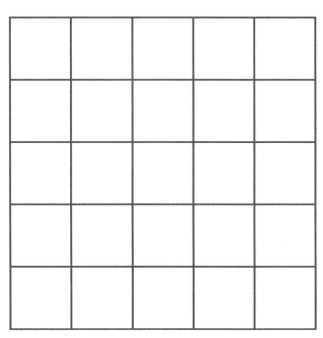

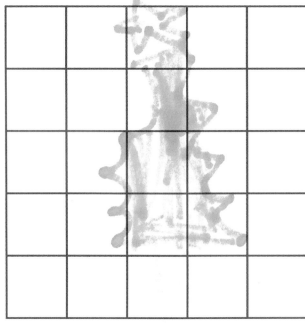

TREE

YOUR TURN TO DRAW

1.

2.

3.

4.

5.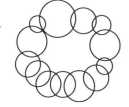

6.

7.

8.

9.

10.

11.

12.

UNICORN

1. 2. 3. 4. 5.

6. 7. 8. 9.

YOUR TURN TO DRAW

PANDA

1.

2.

3.

4.

5.

6.

7.

8.

9.

YOUR TURN TO DRAW ↘

COPY THE COOKIE MAN

VASE

YOUR TURN TO DRAW

1.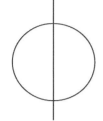

2.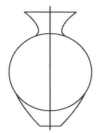

3.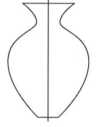

4.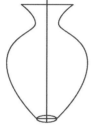

5.

6.

7.

8.

9.

10.

11.

12.

KITTEN

YOUR TURN TO DRAW ↘

1.

2.

3.

4.

5.

6.

7.

8.

9.

LADYBIRD

YOUR TURN TO DRAW ⤵

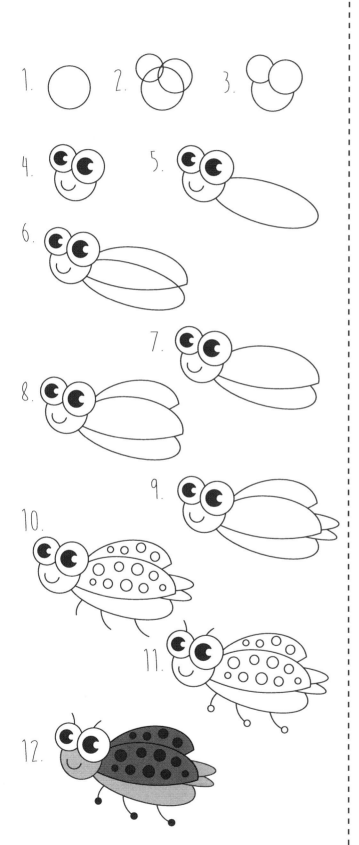

1.
2.
3.
4.
5.
6.
7.
8.
9.
10.
11.
12.

COPY THE CUPCAKE

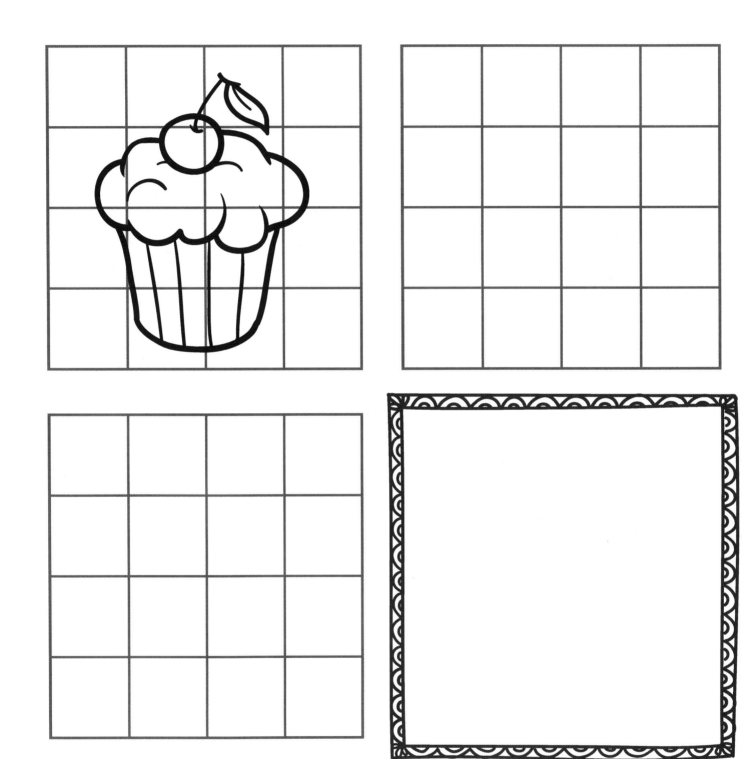

BUNNY

YOUR TURN TO DRAW

HORSE

1.
2.
3.
4.
5.
6.
7.
8.
9.

YOUR TURN TO DRAW

MAI POWNIK

COPY THE ELEPHANT

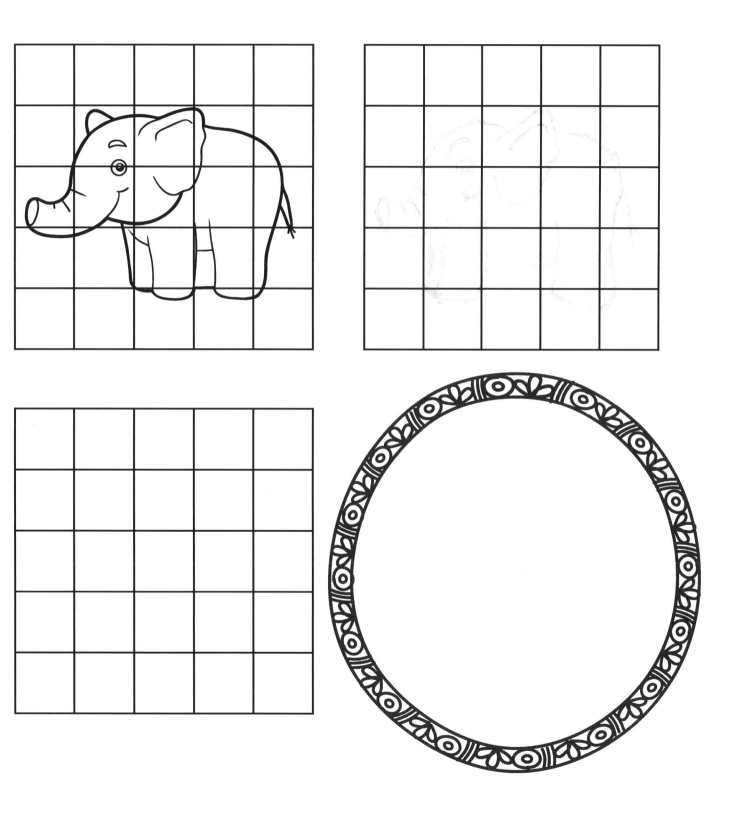

24052384R00037

Printed in Great Britain
by Amazon